UNSCHEDULED FLIGHTS

Unscheduled Flights

Poems
by
JEANETTE MILLER

Adelaide Books
New York/Lisbon
2019

UNSCHEDULED FLIGHTS
Poems
By Jeanette Miller

Copyright © by Jeanette Miller
Cover design © 2019 Adelaide Books

Published by Adelaide Books, New York / Lisbon
adelaidebooks.org

Editor-in-Chief
Stevan V. Nikolic

All rights reserved. No part of this book may be reproduced in any manner whatsoever without written permission from the author except in the case of brief quotations embodied in critical articles and reviews.

For any information, please address Adelaide Books
at info@adelaidebooks.org
or write to:
Adelaide Books
244 Fifth Ave. Suite D27
New York, NY, 10001

ISBN-10: 1-950437-13-2
ISBN-13: 978-1-950437-13-9

Printed in the United States of America

Contents

Rook 11

On The Wall 13

Meeting At George's Bar & Grill 14

Par Avion 15

Persona 16

Three Women: My Apparent Disrespect For Angels . . 17

Revision 18

Year Of The Rooster, Rangoon 19

Daughter Of Shiva 20

The Photographer's Model 21

Just Before Our Break-Up I Dreamed 22

Parallax 23

Rescuer, Recovering 27

Putting My Church Face To Rest 28

Blue Moon 29

Encore For My Aunt 30

Angels Of Feather And Stone 32

And 33

The Deer Of Lake Anita Park 35

Moths	36
A Purchase In India	37
Flight Dreams	38
Holy Water	39
At The Feet Of The Top Of The World	40
Bali, Off-Season	41
Interval	42
In Situ	43
Two Views Of A Photo By Fukase	45
Magritte's Red Curtain	49
Polaroid (Color Composite/Automatic 340)	51
Automat	52
Picking Cherries With A Friend Who's Been Reading Anais Nin	53
Legacy	54
Foreigner	56
I Dream	57
Sextant	58
Refusals	59
The Older Woman	63
In Sequence	64
The Wake	65
When An Old Woman	66
Blue #1	67

UNSCHEDULED FLIGHTS

Edgarly Cemetery 68
Blue #2 69
Eden's Trio 70
Bounty 71
Pods 72
Woman With A Crow 74
Acknowledgments 77
About The Author 81

"One does not always sing out of happiness."

—Pierre Bonnard

ROOK

My metal-fingered rake turns up leaves,
    small twigs and branches, a rusted spoon,
    a piece of blue glass.

Five crows fly toward my house. One
    settles on the roof. The others,
    their wings blue-black as ashes return

to the graveyard four blocks away.
    I've watched them
    high in the pine trees there,

how they circle, naming the stones.
    Ancient Chinese symbols portray crows' legs
    (or wings?) to resemble branches

without leaves, a pictograph read two ways:
    the bird auspicious in front of the sun,
    standing alone – a premonition.

And this lone crow. Why doesn't it fly
    away with the others?
    It's standing like a weathervane

under an overcast sky,
> each eye a window with a separate view.
> I've heard crows can be taught to talk.

If I put a word on its tongue maybe
> I could change my luck. But
> before I can speak, my crow's called

from the air by others of its kind. Together
> they fly above the trees,
> limbs written as birds' wings

connecting two worlds: one where I stand
> without a shadow.
> The crows disappear into the other.

ON THE WALL

Its skirt shaped like a bell,
my wedding dress concealed my body
except for my arms, bare
to lacy, sleeved edges. A veil
distorted my view,
imposing limitations. My father
gave me away. It seemed he, alone,
had made that decision.

I kept the dress in a plastic box
to preserve it forever. Divorced,
I took a scissors to the middle.

Moving from place to place, I lost
the skirt, stretched barbed wire –
a belt across the waist – over what was left.
I framed the specimen under glass.
Its title: Torso Split.

MEETING AT GEORGE'S BAR & GRILL

Our bodies posed across from each other,
we're seated, sculpted figures, more
abstraction than flesh. Unaware,
you're pushing your gold ring
back and forth
across your knuckle. Don't you know
it leaves a pale circle marking your finger?

Neon flickers behind you, alternating
darkness with color, the bulbs
stammering for light. Dividing
our table: a wall like the glass in prisons
separating visitors from the one inside.
This afternoon a deaf mute sold me
a card for a dollar. It illustrated
the alphabet in sign. Your lips
seem to move but I won't hear what you say.
The confident shadow of your wife
claims history, the distance between us.

PAR AVION

Your letters grow fragile
as paper will with age. You dove for mollusks,
covered them with paper, rendering
their shells with lines. I overlapped the envelopes
across my desk – a chain
over the Atlantic. When I spin the globe
its colors blend, come to a stop, true
and separate. Distance is blue.

The locusts protest the night.
Or the inevitable? They must leave
their shells behind. In my drawing
of one of them I erased, to make significant,
the lines left out: No matter how fully
we outline the arc determining
the size of the heart,
like paper valentines, the cut comes next.

PERSONA

When your sister phoned
to report you missing, I invested your departure
with a longing for larger context.
You'd boarded a bus,
leaving old beliefs. After a search
your brother found you, homeless,
committed you to an empty, white room
without sharp objects.
In the hall: a woman who begged me
to open a door
only she could see. You'd created
an image not unlike
your serigraphs of windows
viewed from inside
looking out: your face
in a window as the bus left the station.

THREE WOMEN: MY APPARENT DISRESPECT FOR ANGELS

It is a woman's duty to wear a veil over her head out of regard for the angels.   1st Corinthians 11:11

Mennonite doctrine dictated my father's mother
not to cut her hair. She
wore it coiled, secured in place with hairpins.
Over it: a circular net, gathered and stitched
into a white gauze covering. Obedient,
she pleased the angels.

      Bareheaded, her hair cut and permed, my mother
      defied them but, because she wasn't blood,
      the angels didn't care what she'd done with her hair.

Without scarf or hat, my hair cut short,
I lived outside the blessed. Behind me
like conscience the angry wings of angels scolded.
I searched mirrors
and windows for a glimpse of them
but never saw an angel.

      One Christmas morning a white mist
      spiraled the tree, dropping
      to the carpet below it. Threads
      of spun glass slivered into the soles of my feet
      as I stepped on angels' hair.

REVISION

Snow fell quietly last night, over
well-worn paths, the elms bare
exposing gnarls and hollows,
You left only to return
to repeat your departure. The heart
craves what's familiar,
its particular kind of truth. This time

the air parted behind you, leaving
a wake in your path. You turned to
look back. Did you want me
to follow, as usual, gasping for breath?
This time I stood in place. The air
returned to itself, seamless as water.
This time I didn't call your name.

YEAR OF THE ROOSTER, RANGOON

Burma from the air: a patchwork in military colors.
From the airport tourists go to jail for taking photos
of lined-up soldiers armed with guns.

On the thousand steps to the temple: wares
for sale: the Buddha in every conceivable posture,
woven baskets, carvings, lengths of human hair.

My pale skin drawing stares from children, I leave my shoes
on the bottom step, buy incense, a candle, and
a lotus to offer Buddha. Sitting in silence

he'll remind me not to cling to desire. As I claim my shoes
a boy runs toward me waving
a newspaper. He shouts "Cinema lady is dead!",

repeating this until I buy a paper, find
her photo and death notice in language I can't read
the day Audrey Hepburn died.

DAUGHTER OF SHIVA

A girl of twelve, wearing a gold-threaded sari,
a red dot on your forehead marking
you blessed, you walk in the dusty marketplace,
out of place among the secular beggars. You
beg for rupees to support the temple
of the god with many arms, the long stem
of his metal trident piercing your tongue,
reaching below your chin,
your mouth forced open, speechless.
Did you volunteer for this
sacred mutilation? Or
did the doctrines of elders pierce that emblem
of a god into your tongue?

THE PHOTOGRAPHER'S MODEL

A hard, round lens moved toward me,
        its eye growing smaller
        the closer it came.
You pictured me until the numbers wouldn't escalate
        to hang on a white wall,
        a row of trophies, their corners
securely pinned, the image you desired.
        Drinking wine from paper cups
        people will walk along the frames,
studying them for meaning or beauty. A figure,
        I'm without invitation
        like the glass-eyed doll I loved
in childhood. She sat upright
        and still until
        I laid her down.
Inside her muslin chest: a small, mechanized box
        producing involuntary cries
        someone sewed into her heart.

JUST BEFORE OUR BREAK-UP I DREAMED

An analyst might call it a public dream.
The crowd. The noise.
The commotion. It showed you
as a jester in a prelude
to your act. Your gestures
made music. There were bells
on your coat, your hat.
It was apparent that I was not the only one
who wanted more.
I'd stood in line to buy a ticket
for the dance you'd performed for me
so many times before. In private
charm is potent. Spread thin,
it fades fast.
Oh, the balloons you sent into the air
each time the crowd asked.

PARALLAX

Here's where we part. Without question
you walk your same, sure pace
into the dark, its walls a comfort. Alone
in this difficult light
I'm stumbling
without familiar boundaries.

In the distance ivy adheres
to a wall, an insistent cover of green.
Did you assume I'd continue
to walk beside you, providing
a shadow? I lean into mine as if
it were water. Each movement changes
the shade's configuration. How
we fed each other's hunger for the dark.

"For a woman…transformation is as natural as crossing the street. She stops, walks across, and continues on her way, completely different and yet the same."

—Andrei Sinyavsky (alias, Abram Terts)

RESCUER, RECOVERING

A psychotherapist, I considered it my job
to elevate my clients. "Help me!"
drew me in. I carried them until
my shoulders ached.
What they didn't know: I carried
my own baggage too.
Unconditional compassion
morphed to intermittent tenderness.
Resentment stained assessments.
People = vultures feeding on my spirit.
It eloped. I resigned.

PUTTING MY CHURCH FACE TO REST

After childhood I wore it to the office,
    to parties, to church – too always sweet,
        a gift to lovers
until, tired of repetition, I peeled off layers
    of its applied façade, worn
for approval. Now, when I choose
    to reprise
    my only manner of mask: cosmetic.
I fill in my outlined lips with red, darken
    my lashes, smear shadows across my lids
with the same, studied precision
    my grandfather drew upon.
        The town's undertaker, he worked
        to make up the dead
        to look as they did before dying.

BLUE MOON

Research suggests that high-energy blue wavelengths of
visible light are harmful
as they enter the eye.

———————————————————

A full moon skims the cemetery gate. I try
to preserve it on film but
efforts fail. I'll blame this on
the moonlight. Another moon will rise
before this month ends, then February
without a moon for lovers.

But I'm prepared. Dried luneria occupies
my bedside table, its translucent petals
fragile to touch. Tonight
you took me to a place I'd never been before, I
who'd considered myself a traveler.
You told me if saw blue under my eyelids,
I'd surrendered to love. I saw lavender,
then stars on the ceiling. They shimmered
over us, without expectation.

ENCORE FOR MY AUNT

*"The actors come and go. As they die others are born.
The newborn enters the part vacated by the dead."*
—R.D. Laing

Children inherit the parts of the dead,
an invisible script handed down. I play the role
although the lines belonged to her.
There's little resemblance except for
our hands, the long fingers reaching an octave and two keys.
I see her hands crossing the keyboard
from the lowest bass to highest treble,
and all the keys between,
then folded, rigid as her face, the only visible flesh
on a satin bed. The raised, metal lid.

Hands folded on my lap, I listened
to my mother, her sister,
and their mother – women who were left.
To keep Aunt Helen alive, they
decided I'd major in piano, gave me
a cardboard box filled with her music – chords
like clusters of grapes, ripe and black.

I turned the pages of each book
following signs.
Andante. Allegro. A tempo, hands left over right
for "Buona Notte."
On my piano: her photo recedes behind glass,
my reflection in it
covering the surface of the past.

ANGELS OF FEATHER AND STONE

My mother's mother saved pieces of string,
artificial flowers, and feathers. After her death
my family assembled around her dining table
to divide what she treasured. Burned
as ordinary refuse – string like wick turned to ashes,
plastic flowers melted beyond recognition,
feathers from birds' wings, the spirits
of secular angels
carefully stored in a bureau drawer.

Behind the cemetery walls rise connected houses,
windows facing the backs of graves,
empty as the stare of an angel standing behind her stone.
A man and a woman trim the hedges,
leaves falling to the hem of the angel's gown
where a stain promises to cover
my grandmother's name,
the blades of their shears moving like wings
across the leafy edges.

AND

We lie in bed, every word

      in tandem with the love we make,
      a protest against the dark.

And we'll lie here again tomorrow.

      The dark repeats itself.
      You're at the window

watching

      the snow fall and
      I'm a child again. My father's standing

at the living room window

      staring into distance. He seemed
      to need to look outside. Lured

by a musky scent, I found his footprints

Jeanette Miller

in talcum beside the bath tub
and stepped into them

the same way
I'll track your steps in the snow.

THE DEER OF LAKE ANITA PARK

Framed by the windshield, twelve of them stand,
motionless. Then – in the background –
a subtle movement. A doe approaches the fence.
Her eyes show no fear
although she doesn't know
we're not her enemies.
Even our dog keeps silence.
The brown, stubbled field provides sanctuary
from the killing season. The deer
have nothing to forgive
and nothing to be forgiven for.

MOTHS

It's not the myths that frighten me:
these delicate, white insects
as precursors of death. It's the way
light circling a candle's flame
invites the dark. It asks
for the shadow of their wings
as if radiance were too difficult
like the state of perfection. Tonight
their shadows fall on the porch light.
When I switch it off moths fly
into the dark in search of
another source of light. Someone's turning
to face a window, unaware
of the flutter of wings.

A PURCHASE IN INDIA

This morning, just inside
    Ganesh's temple gate,
    I bought a small, caged bird
    just for the privilege of freeing it to fly.

FLIGHT DREAMS

Hundreds of birds gather in the thorn bushes
every day at five o'clock. They
chatter, even argue the direction they'll take.
The more reluctant hesitate
before they take their place in a formation
above the bridge. Next day they
repeat the maneuver. In dreams I fly,
arms outstretched,
palms down, sometimes a sidewalk below.
A gust of wind lifts me, momentarily
taking my breath. I wonder
why the birds return. Isn't flight enough?
It takes them far beyond the bushes,
their unrelenting brambles.
Tonight, from high altitude,
I understand. Loneliness:
a consequence of continuous fight.

HOLY WATER

An oarsman steers our boat
down the Ganges, cremation fires
on the banks. Below us: bodies of lepers,
victims of smallpox,
and children returned to the mother
of rivers. A boy in a canoe pulls alongside
to sell me a slender, white candle.
It balances on a lotus leaf and floats
away to grant my wish,
its flame disappearing downriver. Which
of the many gods will hear my prayer
in the drone of the holy
reciting mantras in temples risen from water?
Or mourning cries of women hired
to wail over ashes?
Who will notice my candle, insignificant,
compared to fires of the dead?
This boat's gliding slowly between
souls rising in smoke
and those who cling to the river's bed.

AT THE FEET OF THE TOP OF THE WORLD

Sherpas dressed in black wool and
high, black boots, a sash at the waist
holding longknives bargain with vendors
over rugs and chanting bowls.
Women watch from doorways holding
their half-naked babies
while we consult our travel books.

Bearers of *The Lonely Planet*, we
want to believe ourselves capable of
making the long trek
up the blue mountain
but these dark-eyed guides must lead us,
plant the prayer flags,
light our campfires in the snow.

BALI, OFF-SEASON

Artisan studios along narrow roads,
rice-field tiers of green,
pink petals adorning our cottage doorsill reached
from a walk crossing water.
Tiny lizards cling to the ceiling.
Monkeys play on the roof.

On thresholds of cottage doors
dead ancestors leave flowers
and litter the streets with blossoms.

Can a place be too beautiful? A dead dog lies
in a gutter, flies buzzing over
its decaying body. I don't look away.
Praise the dead, this completion.

INTERVAL

I love this quiet between us, each
reading silently. Now
and then you read a line aloud,
words from another world.
Last winter I sent you postcards
from Asia. Each time
I thought of you
I calculated the difference in time.
You were beginning the day
I'd already lived. It seemed the moon
rising over Burma
couldn't have been the one you saw
reflected in the Ohio.
Tonight the pages turn us to
our separate journeys
under a simultaneous moon.

IN SITU

The oak outside our window holds its leaves,

    tintypes
    without faces, ghosts

of other seasons. Lines around your eyes

    mark a past
    I can trace with my finger,

reading in silence like the blind. A gypsy

    once read my palms,
    first the left for possibilities,

the right for completion. You match

    your left palm
    to my right. Bittersweet,

its orange craters repeated in the mirror, –
    two views
    of the same array, one so close

it can be touched, the other

an image of what's within our vision,
beautiful,

not easily grasped. The light beyond the oak

takes its shape forming
a pattern on my neighbor's house.

What if I followed the pattern, painted the shadows?

I could order it,
own it. The light

would fill the places I'd made for it until it stole

into the afternoon,
its movements unseen

as an hour's hand, leaving time

a marked absence behind
to appear the next day

gold spilled over its boundaries, its shape altered,
elusive as the crescent of light
reflected from your coffee cup. It flew

from the wall to the ceiling

settled on the table,
shimmering, changing shape in my hand.

TWO VIEWS OF A PHOTO BY FUKASE

A solitary crow, one wing upturned
like open fingers,
the other a chord of treble notes, its feathers
erased by the wind. The bird
becomes flight, transcending itself like time
wedged between the numbers on a clock, extending outward
beyond measure. Making love, we forget limitations
of body. We're not ourselves but love.

Snow. The fanned wing descends in white,
the crow a figure absence magnifies.
Outside my window: tree limbs profiled by sky
between them. My form's defined by hours
alone. This morning,
driving back from your apartment,
I swerved to keep from hitting a crow.
It receded in my rear-view mirror
to a black point where I'd turned
to cross the white line, the wheel in my hands.

"Poets don't carry pens but writers do."

—Jean Cocteau

MAGRITTE'S RED CURTAIN

a villanelle on "Decalcomania"

The muse becomes a man with clouds in his head.
She parts the red curtain and appears at night.

She remains with him until his words are said.
She had lured him from the comfort of his bed
to stand at the window, preparing for flight.

The muse becomes a man with clouds in his head,
entering his thoughts, transforming them instead
into the poems she urges him to write

and remains with him until his words are said.

He picks up his pen, unaware she has fled.
He's focused on lines that move across the white.
The muse becomes a man with clouds in his head.

She doesn't return if enough dreams are read,
if he walks in them – a necessary rite.
She remains with him until his words are said.

Jeanette Miller

He sees her eyes in his mirror. She has led
him to this impression, his face in the light.

The muse becomes a man with clouds in his head.
She stayed with him until the poems were said.

POLAROID
(Color Composite/Automatic 340)

Because the old Land camera is an archaic model
and I'm not accustomed
to tugging at a cardboard tab to open a plastic door
that lets the picture exit,
then waiting 60 seconds
before removing the protective layer of paper,
the image of my mother
bent over her garden this morning,
her round, straw hat in the foreground,
is nothing but darkness, a yellow ring
fading to black, but
the sun burning through the walnut trees
comes up the size of a coin.
It stays. Waiting is one way to revise.

AUTOMAT

on the painting by Edward Hopper, 1927

Two rows of lights reflect in a window
of an all-night restaurant,
a bowl of ripe fruit on the sill.
Eyelids lowered, her legs crossed, a woman,
alone, looks into her coffee cup,
reading its contents. One of her hands
holds its handle,
the other hand gloved.
What brought her to this place,
this kind of isolation?
She doesn't seem abandoned.
She's not waiting for someone but
something undefined. She listens
to her selective and solitary heart
as shadows occupy the room, disappearing
like the past in morning's light.

PICKING CHERRIES WITH A FRIEND WHO'S BEEN READING ANAIS NIN

after re-reading Robert Hass

Dried summer mud glazes the road.
We drive to an orchard, stopped
by its barbed-wire boundary, park
along the ditch and find a locked gate.
Persevering, Lisa tosses a pail
between the lines, crawls under the fence
and I follow. After filling our pail
I climb to reach the higher branches,
shaking cherries into her skirt.
At the base of the tree: a dead sparrow.
In tears, her skirt stained red, Lisa
runs back to the car, spilling cherries
destined to waste, and
cradles herself in a bucket seat.

LEGACY

Snakes held high, holy women danced
the change of seasons and
priestesses served the temples, their bodies
a liaison between heaven and earth.

Trees absorbed light, printing themselves
in shadow and God walked, transitive,
through the garden where
lilies opened their six, orange tongues.

At the base of a tree a snake
shed its skin,
then crawled into the branches. It spoke
with fire in its mouth
in words the woman understood. But
she put aside this knowledge
to name with the man, their lives
a finite number of breaths.

Assuming the power to name, he worded
the rivers, mountains, the sky. Into the night

they named, forgetting the landscape
of their dreaming with no horizon line.

The snake crawled away
to live outside language, emerging
at night in vines replicating its form. Leaves
surrounded the lilies, slender phrases
hidden inside their folded tongues.

FOREIGNER

"Writer's block is the unconscious making its secret preparations."
—Louise Bogan

From inside, their umbrellas turning
in steady rain, people walking King George Street
seem curious fish, their noses pressed
against aquarium glass. They peer
to see if this old pub's still
serving beer. *Saloon Bar. Public Bar.* These signs
once divided lower from upper class.
Today the building calls for words. Manuscripts
fall through the door slot, requests
for Anvil Press to publish. Poets
sat round a collating table last night
telling stories after dinner. I touched my throat
like I'd press a plate for bread crumbs,
searching for unspoken words.

I DREAM

I 'm falling through clouds
but can't reach Earth. Cars, buses
above and below.

Monkeys, toucans, rows
of palm trees and a flower
becoming an egg.

Kimonos printed
with rain, paper cranes, gates to
repeating heavens.

SEXTANT

for Peter Jay

We walked along a pebbled beach
in Suffolk. Pointing to a signpost
you read "Minsmere."
Because I'd turned away or
because the gulls' cries filled the air
I heard *wind's mirror.*
But the wind isn't vain. It
doesn't look to the sea
for a reflection. It exists
in what it moves – boats drifting
from their towlines, empty fishing nets.
Wind blows your hair as you walk,
the sky and sea dividing blue.
An instrument, a meridian, you
mark the distance
between us and the stars.

REFUSALS

                    after watching Jean Cocteau's film, "Orphee"

Death calls him from the mirror.
Orpheus can't reach her,
alive. But he's a poet; the mirror
remains only mirror until
he puts on his gloves. Hands first,

                he passes through the glass, becoming
                Death's lover. Mortal, he longs for
                what he doesn't have: Eurydice, her body.

Orpheus wants both women but Death
demands he choose. You know the rest.
She watches him turn,
the mirror revealing the fatal gesture.

                He exits alone. On the other side Eurydice
                is dead. He pushes against
                a thick wall of glass, the void unbearable,
                as an empty page
                on which no words assemble.

"... after the moon has turned old... it is the same hunt, but in different shadows, under different trees."

—W.S. Merwin, from The Lost Upland

THE OLDER WOMAN

What can I give you but this used pear
spent of another man's namesake,
foreigners to our bed. Not content
with my love you want
children of your own. This chasm
separates us, giving weight to every word
and gesture. You describe a garden
where we could walk
among the sculptures, a statue of lovers there
in permanent embrace. Time
can't touch them, their love set in stone
but it robbed us
of the years between us. Look.
Already our shadows have moved
past the replica of lovers.

IN SEQUENCE

for Katie Waters

I received your postcard depicting a painting
of old women, *Der Jungbrunnen* brought by horse cart
to a rectangular pool. They submerge
on the left, emerge on the right, young, beautiful, naked.

A woman who no longer bleeds,
I'm long past the desire
for childbirth. A crone's emerging
in my mirror. I smooth oil under her eyes
and, periodically,
pull brittle white hairs from my chin. It's time
to remove dry stalks
from my garden. Their roots
will lie dormant
until they re-invent themselves.

THE WAKE

December's end in Iowa, my car doors frozen shut.
At the mortuary
my four-year old granddaughter asked
"Is she wearing shoes?"
The funeral director lifted the closed half
of the casket's lid
to show Pauline her great-grandmother's feet
seen through transparent nylon.

My ex-mother-in-law rested, dressed
in lavender silk, one hand over the other,
her weddings rings
not visible. I stood in line
to shake hands with former family
except for my ex-husband, then
made my exit. Our hands
would have joined us
to long-buried associations.

WHEN AN OLD WOMAN

takes a young companion she finds
more than her youth, his taut skin
and quick step. A chance
to begin again. An elderly painter loved
a potter young enough
to be her grandson. He taught her
a new dimension, art she could shape in her hands.
Her brushes went untouched. In time
he left her but not without guilt. He doubted
she could spin the wheel
without him, imagined
her standing alone in the desert
facing clouds, a dark and lonely figure
against sky. This: his illusion.
She filled her studio with new canvases, rows
of bowls and urns. A large canvas
duplicated the window of one adobe wall.
Purple horizon lines.
Above them sun. Solitary. Brilliant.

BLUE #1

My friend and I cleared out the apartment
of her mother's Russian boyfriend,
finding, on a closet shelf,
a child's blue swim trunks
shrunken the way wool responds to water
and,
in a cardboard box: a photo of a boy
beside a small boat, in each hand an oar.
A translator of the words
handwritten on the back
helped us understand the boat had capsized.
Did Vladimer's son, Alexis, lose the oars
or were they still in his hands when he drowned?

EDGARLY CEMETERY

It's the fifth month when the living
    remember their dead, offering
    wreaths and baskets of flowers. Some plant perennials
    for more permanent tribute. Trees blossom overhead.
The gateway's arch, erected
    to honor Union soldiers, interrupts
    an iron fence along the sidewalk, a mausoleum's doorway
    long closed by a mound of earth.
A block away the stones diminish
    to tablets, capsules. On my balcony
    a red-orange hibiscus opens
    every few weeks in a shrill
of color. It holds this position for days, then closes
    to itself At day's end, quieted by stillness,
    a cup of tea in hand, I locate myself
    between short-lived blooms and
                    all that distant flowering.

BLUE #2

In just four days a bacteria subtracted
    my granddaughter's breath. Her parents
    planted a garden of flowers known
    to attract butterflies and I asked

a tattoo artist to angle, diagonally, a blue butterfly
    poised to lift in flight
    from my shoulder.
    The voices of children call me

to raise my eyes from this page. A playground.
    A boy and girl dancing
    under a continuous arc of water,
    the girl about the age Ivy would have turned

this year. In a rush of blue a motorcycle blurs
    the nearby highway. A neon café sign flashes
    blue: OPEN   OPEN   OPEN   OPEN   OPEN

EDEN'S TRIO

He was designed to care for the garden.
It was lonely work. Contributing
to his distress, incompletion
possessed him. Eventually presented
with a body like his, not like his,
he partnered. From her beginnings,
she knew they couldn't sustain
the honeymoon. Enter the snake
we were taught to blame.
"You must not lose yourself
in that party of two," it whispered. In accord
with the serpent, the woman
decided to offer the man its advice, presented
with an apple slice. She
made her deadline just in time. In three months
their relationship had turned into
a hothouse of unattainable expectations.

BOUNTY

For more abundant growth,
my neighbor advised me
to pinch off the basil's flowers, this process
eliminating
what I'd once thought beautiful,
not unlike the rituals
performed by my mirror
for seven decades.

The garden I planted went to seed
because I neglected it
for other projects. Some plants
made domes. Others stemmed
over three feet tall,
their petals falling to the ground
like snow. Such unattended beauty,
the unpredictable form.

PODS

I.
Some thing pushes from inside
to form waves
on the shells, secrets
lying dormant for the cold season.
Connected to their casings: twigs
marked with antlers
that one day will protrude the skin,
imitating those that hold them,
each pod a wingless bird
of weathered bronze. See
how their beaks curve
toward earth. One splits open, its tongue
a seed fastened by a wire
to a gauze lining. Some seeds
become tribal masks without eyes,
no mouths, only profiles
facing each other or clay heads
propped against a white wall.

II.
The pods split open as if sliced along lines
drawn in brown pencil, eels gliding

below the desk lamp, casting shadows
on a surface of light.

III.
Tonight I can wait no longer.
The pods crack when I pull them
apart, seeds rolling
the length of the lining, still attached.
Removed from their stems
they lie, opened.
To crush them would be a brittle act.

WOMAN WITH A CROW

Loving the darkness she holds
in her hands, she
strokes its breast. The crow rests,
not turning its head. They
face the same direction.
She draws the bird to the fold
of her bodice, her palm against
its feathered pulse.

Picasso painted the shoulders
of this dark-haired woman
high and narrow to resemble wings,
raised unnaturally. Why
do we impose on birds the burden
of carrying our dreams of flight?
Maybe she holds the crow too close.

Thank you to the Iowa Arts Council for funding the cost of editing via an Individual Artist's grant and heartfelt thanks to my editor, April Ossmann, who led me to a larger view of this manuscript. Thanks also to readers, Jan Weissmiller, Claudia Bischoff, Phil Kemp, Sandy Kemp, Ann Khan, Anne Gregory, Diane Flynn, Marc Van Alstein, and a special thank you to Igor Savelev who, over the years, encouraged me to continue writing when I felt like giving up.

Acknowledgments

Phoebe
    Bali, Off-season

Shenandoah
    Magritte's Red Curtain

Caesura
    Two Views of a Photo by Fukase

Poet & Critic
    Encore For My Aunt
    Cyclical
    Woman With a Crow
    Pods
    And

Iowa Journal of Literary Studies
    In situ

Prairie Schooner
    Sextant
    Parallax

Southern Indiana Review
Flight Dreams
Year of the Rooster

Wapsipinicon Almanac
The Deer of Lake Anita Park

WordWrights
When An Old Woman

The Comstock Review
Legacy

Pegasus
Interval

Colere
At the Feet of the Top of the World

The Flying Island
The Photographer's Model

Main Street Rag anthology, Of Burgers & Barrooms
Our Meeting at George's Bar & Grill
Foreigner in Greenwich

Des Moines Art Center anthology
Automat

WAVES: a Confluence of Women's Voices anthology
 Parallax
 The Photographer's Model

About the Author

A graduate of the Iowa Writer's Workshop, Jeanette Miller is now retired after teaching creative writing at Scattergood Friend's School, a Quaker-founded boarding high school in West Branch, Iowa and, as an adjunct professor, at the University of Southern Indiana in Evansville.

She also worked as a mental health counselor in not-for-profit clinics in Iowa after earning her MA in Counseling Psychology at Marymount University in Arlington, VA.

Jeanette currently lives in downtown Iowa City with her cat, Merci and is working on a memoir about the years she was primary caregiver for her aging parents.

www.ingramcontent.com/pod-product-compliance
Lightning Source LLC
Chambersburg PA
CBHW020730100426
42735CB00038B/1663